WORKBOOK FOR

RANGE

Why Generalists Triumph In A Specialized World

Book Spark

This workbook is an unofficial companion and is not endorsed or created by the author of the original book. The content and opinions within are derived from independent research and expertise. Although every attempt has been made to maintain accuracy, the author and publisher absolve themselves of responsibility for any inaccuracies or omissions. Readers are advised to cross-reference information with additional sources.

This workbook is not intended to be a substitute for professional advice, diagnosis, or treatment.

TABLE OF CONTENTS

WORKBOOK OVERVIEW

✱✱✱

Unlock the secrets of David J. Epstein's book with this interactive workbook!

This workbook is your guide to a deeper understanding of David J. Epstein's book. Follow these steps to get the most out of it and apply the concepts to your life:

1. Get the big picture. Read the chapter summary in this workbook to understand the books main themes and ideas.

2. Read the original work. Once you have a general understanding of the book, dive into the original text. The details will be easier to grasp with the big picture in mind.

3. Apply the concepts. Once you have a solid understanding of the core concepts, start working through the exercises in this workbook.

4. Put it into practice. The exercises in this workbook are designed to help you apply the main concepts to your life.

To assist you with applying the main concepts, the following exercises are present:

- Key takeaways: Summarize the main points of each chapter to help you focus on the most important topics.
- Reflective questions: Reflect on your own experiences and identify areas where you can apply the concepts to change your life. Write your thoughts in the workbook.
- Action steps: Develop practical steps to take action and improve your life.
- Self-assessments: Evaluate your progress and identify areas where you need to continue working.

THINK before you DO! This is the key to making lasting changes in your life.

P.S. Remember to leave a review! Every review helps us to create better workbooks for readers.

INTRODUCTION

✳✳✳

Chapter Summary

The Paradox Of Specialization: Embracing Breadth In A Specialized World

ROGER FEDERER'S DIVERSE athletic upbringing, encompassing multiple sports, contributed to his exceptional hand-eye coordination and athleticism. His father believed this broad exposure would lead to greater impact than renowned figures like Mandela, Gandhi, or Buddha.

In contrast, Tiger Woods' upbringing focused on early and narrow specialization in golf, epitomized by the "ten-thousand-hours rule" of deliberate practice. This approach has shaped popular beliefs about skill development, emphasizing intense focus on a single domain.

However, research suggests that elite athletes at the pinnacle of their skills actually devote more time to focused, purposeful practice than their near-elite counterparts. This challenges the notion that early and narrow specialization is always the key to success.

Beyond sports, hyperspecialization has become a prominent marketing technique, with individuals often prioritizing depth over breadth. While early specialization can lead to higher earnings after college, later specialists may find jobs that better suit their skills and dispositions.

Notable figures like Duke Ellington and Maryam Mirzakhani exemplify the benefits of gaining knowledge in various fields, trading depth for breadth as their careers progressed. Military veterans, who often become specialists later in life, also face challenges in job advancement due to their diverse experiences.

The author emphasizes the importance of expanding personal and professional horizons, acknowledging that it takes time and requires a head start. They argue that highly specialized experts can become narrow-minded and worsen with experience, while slow learning is optimal for accumulating long-term knowledge.

Overspecialization can lead to collective problems as well. The 2008 financial crisis exposed the dangers of segregation within large banks, and overspecialization in healthcare can result in a narrow focus on specific treatments.

The challenge is to sustain the benefits of breadth, broad experience, interdisciplinary thinking, and delayed concentration in a world that increasingly rewards hyperspecialization. As complexity grows, we need more "Rogers"—individuals who begin broad and welcome varied experiences and opinions as they mature.

Key Takeaways And Learning

1. Roger Federer's upbringing in an athletic household and his father's belief in his abilities contributed to his success.

2. Tiger Woods and Roger Federer's early friendship and rivalry highlighted the importance of deliberate practice and focused training.

3. Early sampling and diversity in skill development can lead to greater success and job satisfaction later in life.

4. Hyperspecialization is often marketed as a key to success, but it can limit one's potential and lead to narrow-mindedness.

5. Slow learning and delayed concentration can be beneficial for accumulating long-term knowledge and expertise.

6. Overspecialization can lead to collective tragedy, as seen in the 2008 financial crisis and in healthcare systems.

7. It is important to sustain the benefits of breadth, broad experience, interdisciplinary thinking, and delayed concentration in a world that increasingly rewards hyperspecialization.

8. As complexity grows, we need more "Rogers" – people who begin broad and welcome varied experiences and opinions as they mature.

Questions To Think About

1. How do you think your upbringing has influenced your interests and skills?

_____

_____

_____

_____

_____

_____

_____

2. Do you believe that early specialization is necessary for success in sports or other fields?

_____

_____

_____

_____

_____

_____

_____

3. What are the potential benefits of pursuing a diverse range of interests and activities?

_____

_____

_____

_____

_____

_____

_____

4. How can you maintain the benefits of breadth, broad experience, interdisciplinary thinking, and delayed concentration in a world that increasingly rewards hyperspecialization?

_____

_____

_____

_____

_____

_____

_____

5. Do you think that the pressure to specialize early and narrowly is beneficial or harmful?

_____

_____

_____

_____

_____

_____

_____

6. What are some examples of notable people who have benefited from a diverse range of experiences and interests?

_____

_____

_____

_____

_____

_____

_____

7. How can we encourage more people to embrace diversity and delayed specialization?

_____

_____

_____

_____

_____

_____

_____

8. What are some of the risks associated with overspecialization in different fields?

_____

_____

_____

_____

_____

_____

_____

9. How can we create systems and institutions that support and reward breadth and interdisciplinary thinking?

_____

_____

_____

_____

_____

_____

_____

10. What are some strategies for individuals to maintain a broad perspective and continue learning throughout their careers?

Personal Growth Activities

1. Embracing Diversity In Early Development:

• *Action:*

Encourage children to participate in a variety of sports, activities, and learning experiences, rather than focusing solely on one area of specialization.

• *Exercise:*

Create a schedule that allows your child to explore different interests, whether it's sports, music, art, science, or language.

• *Analysis:*

Observe your child's progress and interests. Are they showing a natural aptitude or passion for a particular activity? Encourage them to continue exploring and developing their skills while still maintaining a diverse range of interests.

2. Balancing Specialization And Breadth In Education And Career:

• *Action:*

Seek out educational programs and career paths that offer a broad foundation of knowledge and skills, along with opportunities for specialization later on.

• *Exercise:*

Research different majors and career fields that align with your interests and goals. Consider programs that offer interdisciplinary studies, minors, or opportunities to explore different areas before committing to a specific specialization.

• *Analysis:*

Evaluate your skills, interests, and values. Identify areas where you excel and enjoy learning, and consider how you can apply those strengths to a career that offers both depth and breadth.

3. Promoting Interdisciplinary Thinking And Collaboration:

• *Action:*

Foster a culture of interdisciplinary thinking and collaboration in your workplace or community. Encourage individuals from different fields and backgrounds to share their perspectives and work together on projects.

• *Exercise:*

Organize events, workshops, or discussion groups that bring together people from diverse backgrounds to share their knowledge and expertise.

• *Analysis:*

Observe the outcomes of interdisciplinary collaboration. Did the diverse perspectives and skills lead to innovative solutions or improved decision-making? How can you continue to promote and support interdisciplinary collaboration in your organization or community?

Motivation

"The broader you are, the better you are."

CHAPTER 1

✳✳✳

Chapter Summary

The Limits Of Specialization: Expertise Vs. Adaptability In A Complex World

LASZLO POLGAR'S EXPERIMENT in homeschooling his daughters to become chess prodigies illustrates the power of early specialization and pattern recognition. However, studies by Gary Klein and Daniel Kahneman reveal that expertise in specific domains can lead to overconfidence and decreased adaptability in unfamiliar situations.

Machines excel at tactical tasks, while humans excel at strategic thinking and adaptability. This was evident in the "advanced chess" and "freestyle chess" competitions, where human-computer teams outperformed grandmasters.

The concept of "chunking" in chess demonstrates how experts can quickly recognize and recreate complex patterns. However, this specialization comes at a cost: those who don't begin intense training by age twelve have significantly lower chances of becoming international masters.

Savants and AI systems thrive in structured, rule-bound environments. However, in open-ended, unpredictable situations, they struggle. This is because they rely on established patterns that may not apply in novel contexts.

The Polgar sisters' success and Tiger Woods' dominance in golf have led to popular analogies about the importance of early specialization. However, these analogies overlook the fact that many successful individuals have diverse interests and are able to adapt to changing circumstances.

In complex, "wicked" environments, adaptability and range are more valuable than narrow specialization. Creative achievers often draw insights from multiple disciplines, allowing them to see connections and patterns that others miss.

The belief that expertise is always acquired in a "kind" learning environment is a misconception. In many fields, including medicine and business, the rules are constantly changing, and professionals must learn to adapt and unlearn.

While specialization can lead to expertise in a narrow domain, it can also limit adaptability and creativity. In a rapidly changing world, individuals with a broad range of interests and the ability to transfer knowledge across domains are more likely to succeed.

Key Takeaways And Learning

1. Laszlo Polgar believed that traditional education was broken and that he could turn his children into geniuses through early education and homeschooling.

2. The Polgar sisters, Susan, Sofia, and Judit, became brilliant chess players and the first women to qualify for the men's world championship and earn grandmaster status through tournament play against males.

3. Psychologists Gary Klein and Daniel Kahneman discovered that professionals in various domains, including chess masters, instantly recognize familiar patterns.

4. Highly trained professionals frequently develop confidence but not skill as a result of their experience.

5. In "kind" learning environments, patterns recur over and over, and feedback is exceedingly accurate and typically swift.

6. In "wicked" learning environments, game rules are frequently ambiguous or partial, recurrent patterns may or may not exist, and feedback is frequently delayed, incorrect, or both.

7. Experience in wicked learning environments can reinforce the wrong lessons.

8. Machines and humans frequently have opposing strengths and limitations.

9. The Moravec paradox states that machines are tactically faultless when compared against humans.

10. Chunking is a technique used in chess to quickly recreate a game board after only three seconds of viewing it.

11. Early training in technical practice is essential for chess players to develop chunking skills.

12. Savants have abilities in a particular domain that considerably exceed their abilities in others.

13. AI has made great progress in various computer games but struggles in confined, rule-bound settings and open-ended situations.

14. The mistaken belief that human skill is always acquired in an extraordinarily kind learning environment is a misunderstanding.

15. Specialisation in a restricted and specialised field is not the key to inventive performance.

16. Creative achievers have a wide range of interests, which allows them to provide insights that cannot be attributed solely to domain-specific expertise.

17. Successful adapters excel in transferring knowledge from one endeavor to another in a creative way while avoiding cognitive entrenchment.

18. In a wicked world with ill-defined obstacles and few rigid rules, range can be a game changer.

Questions To Think About

1. What are your thoughts on Laszlo Polgar's belief that traditional education was broken and that he could turn his children into geniuses by giving them a good head start?

_____

_____

_____

_____

_____

_____

_____

2. Do you agree that experience inevitably leads to competence, or do you think that it depends on the topic in question?

_____

_____

_____

_____

_____

_____

_____

3. What are some examples of "kind" learning environments, and how do they differ from "wicked" learning environments?

_____

_____

_____

_____

_____

_____

_____

4. What is the Moravec paradox, and how does it relate to the strengths and limitations of machines and humans in different domains?

_____

_____

_____

_____

_____

_____

_____

5. What is "chunking," and how does it help to explain instances of miraculous, domain-specific memory?

_____
_____
_____
_____
_____
_____
_____

6. Why do you think that AI systems, like savants, require consistent architecture and limited environments?

_____
_____
_____
_____
_____
_____
_____

7. What are some examples of "Martian tennis" in the business world, and how can businesses learn to thrive in these unpredictable environments?

_____
_____
_____
_____
_____

_____

_____

8. Do you agree that specialization in a restricted and specialized field is not the key to inventive performance?

_____

_____

_____

_____

_____

_____

_____

Why or why not?

_____

_____

_____

_____

_____

_____

_____

9. What are some examples of creative achievers who have a wide range of interests, and how has this helped them to achieve success?

_____

_____

_____

_____

_____

_____

_____

10. How can individuals avoid cognitive entrenchment and become successful adapters in a rapidly changing world?

_____

_____

_____

_____

_____

_____

_____

Personal Growth Activities

1. Pattern Recognition And Chunking:

• *Action:*

Practice pattern recognition and chunking exercises to improve your ability to identify and remember complex information quickly.

• *Exercise:*

Play a game of chess or another strategy game, focusing on memorizing the positions of pieces and identifying patterns in your opponent's moves. Try to chunk information into meaningful groups, like groups of pieces or sequences of moves.

• *Analysis:*

Reflect on how chunking helped you remember information more effectively. Did it make it easier to recall specific details or make strategic decisions?

2. Embracing Range And Adaptability:

• *Action:*

Seek out experiences and activities that challenge your existing skills and knowledge, pushing you to learn and adapt in new ways.

• *Exercise:*

Take a class in a subject you know little about, try a new sport or hobby, or travel to a place with a different culture. Pay attention to how you learn and adapt in these new situations.

• *Analysis:*

Reflect on how your experiences outside your comfort zone have influenced your thinking and problem-solving abilities. Did they help you develop a broader perspective or become more flexible in your approach to learning?

3. Creative Problem-Solving And Transfer Of Knowledge:

• *Action:*

Engage in creative problem-solving activities that require you to apply knowledge from different domains or disciplines.

• *Exercise:*

Try solving a puzzle or riddle that requires you to think outside the box. Work on a project that combines different skills and interests, such as writing a story that incorporates scientific concepts or creating a piece of art inspired by a historical event.

• *Analysis:*

Reflect on how you were able to transfer knowledge from one domain to another. Did your diverse experiences and interests help you come up with unique and innovative solutions?

Motivation

"In a wicked world with ill-defined obstacles and few rigid rules, range can be a game changer."

CHAPTER 2

✳✳✳

Chapter Summary

The Flynn Effect And Its Implications

THE FLYNN EFFECT is the phenomenon of average scores on IQ tests increasing with each new generation. This has been observed in many countries over the past century. Standardized IQ tests, with an average score of 100, have been instrumental in identifying this trend.

Factors Driving The Flynn Effect

- Modernization and Access to Education:

Modernization, increased access to education, and exposure to modern air and nutrition have contributed to the development of problem-solving abilities, particularly abstract thinking, in children.

- Socioeconomic Progress:

The Industrial Revolution, the emergence of cities, and the development of a global economy have created more abstract concepts, leading to changes in how people process information.

- Changing Employment Structures:

Research studies have shown that individuals in rural areas who adopt modern employment practices demonstrate increased abstract thinking.

- Scientific Frameworks:

Modern individuals rely on abstract concepts and frameworks to organize information, allowing for the transfer of knowledge between fields.

- Transferable Skills from Modern Work:

Modern work and self-directed problem-solving have been linked to higher scores on IQ tests in individuals from six industrializing countries.

- Women's Changing Roles:

Women in traditional religious societies have experienced a more pronounced Flynn effect due to the expansion of their roles and increased access to modern education.

Limitations Of The Flynn Effect

- Overemphasis on Specialization:

Society has prioritized specialization over conceptual, transferable knowledge, leading to a negative correlation between GPA and scores on tests of broad conceptual thinking.

- Lack of Generalizable Knowledge:

Specialized education often results in individuals being unable to apply their knowledge to new situations or across fields.

The Importance Of Broad Thinking Skills

- Adaptability:

Broad thinking skills, including the ability to switch between categories and create new categories, are essential in a rapidly changing world.

- Applying Knowledge Across Fields:

The ability to apply knowledge across fields stems from extensive training in conceptual reasoning, enabling researchers to become experts in various fields.

The author emphasizes the importance of conceptual reasoning skills in a changing world, highlighting the need for individuals to develop broad thinking tools and the ability to transfer knowledge between fields.

Key Takeaways And Learning

1. The Flynn effect is a phenomenon in which correct IQ test responses increased with each new generation over the twentieth century.

2. The Flynn effect is due to the standardized character of IQ tests, which have an average score of 100 points.

3. The Progressive Matrices, a mathematical tool, has resulted in significant improvements in children's problem-solving ability.

4. The Soviet Union's socialist revolution transformed agricultural land into enormous collective farms and accelerated industrial development, resulting in networked economies and the development of a system for matching symbols to sounds.

5. Remote villagers are less prone to optical illusions than industrialized world dwellers because they are not as attuned to the holistic environment.

6. Exposure to modern work and self-directed problem-solving has been associated with cognitive flexibility in individuals in six industrializing countries.

7. Modern minds are more adaptable, allowing individuals to consider complicated situations and draw connections across multiple fields.

8. The Flynn effect has been experienced more gradually by women in traditional religious societies.

9. Society has historically prioritized specialization over conceptual, transferable knowledge.

10. There is no evidence that any department strives to create anything other than restricted key competencies.

11. Broad thinking tools, such as Fermi-izing, can be used across fields.

12. Conceptual reasoning skills are critical for linking new ideas and working across contexts.

13. The ability to apply knowledge broadly stems from extensive training.

14. Researchers who learn to apply information extensively can become better researchers in a variety of fields.

Questions To Think About

1. What evidence supports the Flynn effect?

_____

_____

_____

_____

_____

_____

_____

2. What is the Flynn effect and how is it measured?

_____

_____

_____

_____

_____

_____

_____

3. What are some of the factors that have been linked to the Flynn effect?

_____

_____

_____

_____

_____

_____

_____

4. How does the Flynn effect impact different groups of people?

_____

_____

_____

_____

_____

_____

_____

5. What are some of the implications of the Flynn effect for education and society?

_____

_____

_____

_____

_____

_____

_____

6. What are some of the challenges to promoting conceptual reasoning and transferable knowledge in education?

_____

_____

_____

_____

_____

_____

_____

7. What are some examples of how conceptual reasoning and transferable knowledge can be used in different fields?

_____

_____

_____

_____

_____

_____

_____

8. How can we develop our own conceptual reasoning and transferable knowledge skills?

_____

_____

_____

_____

_____

_____

_____

9. What are some of the benefits of having strong conceptual reasoning and transferable knowledge skills?

_____

_____

_____

_____

_____

_____

10. How can we create learning environments that promote conceptual reasoning and transferable knowledge?

_____

_____

_____

_____

_____

_____

_____

Personal Growth Activities

1. Embracing Abstract Thinking:

• *Action:*

Engage in activities that challenge your abstract thinking skills, such as solving puzzles, playing strategy games, or learning a new language.

• *Exercise:*

Try completing a logic puzzle or a Sudoku game. Alternatively, play a game of chess or Go, where strategic thinking is essential. You could also start learning a new language, which requires you to think in abstract ways to understand grammar and vocabulary.

• *Analysis:*

Reflect on your experience. Did you find these activities challenging or enjoyable? Did you notice any improvements in your abstract thinking abilities over time?

2. Cross-Disciplinary Knowledge Application:

• *Action:*

Seek opportunities to apply knowledge and skills from one field to another. This could involve reading books or articles outside your usual领域participating in interdisciplinary projects, or taking online courses in different subjects.

• *Exercise:*

Choose a topic that interests you and explore it from multiple perspectives. For example, if you're interested in history, you could read books on the history of science, art, and politics related to that period. Or, if you're studying biology, you could explore how biological principles apply to fields like psychology, engineering, or computer science.

• *Analysis:*

Reflect on your experience. Did you find it challenging or rewarding to apply knowledge across different fields? Did you discover new connections or insights?

3. Developing Conceptual Reasoning Skills:

• *Action:*

Engage in activities that require you to think conceptually and make connections between different pieces of information. This could involve reading philosophical texts, writing essays, or participating in debates.

• *Exercise:*

Read a philosophical essay or book and try to identify the main arguments and concepts. Write an essay on a topic that requires you to synthesize information from multiple sources. Or, participate in a debate or discussion where you need to defend your position using logical arguments.

• *Analysis:*

Reflect on your experience. Did you find these activities challenging or enjoyable? Did you notice any improvements in your conceptual reasoning abilities over time?

Motivation

"The greatest glory in living lies not in never falling, but in rising every time we fall." • Nelson Mandela

CHAPTER 3

***

Chapter Summary

The Enigmatic World Of Musical Mastery

IN 17TH-CENTURY VENICE, instrumental music underwent a major transformation, giving rise to new instruments, established musical keys, and virtuoso performers. The concerto emerged, with Antonio Vivaldi as its undisputed master. The all-female figlie del coro captivated audiences across Europe, attracting royalty and nobility.

These talented women, often born to mothers working in Venice's sex industry, found refuge and musical education at the Ospedale della Pietà, a charitable institution. Under strict discipline, they honed their skills, becoming multi-instrumentalists and performing a wide range of music.

The figlie del coro's success sparked interest in the secrets of musical mastery. Parents and the media sought formulas for raising child prodigies, often emphasizing early specialization and intense practice. However, research suggests that the path to musical excellence is less straightforward.

Studies have shown that the amount of practice time alone is not a reliable predictor of musical success. Instead, a diverse musical background, including exposure to multiple instruments, seems to be more beneficial.

Exceptional musicians like Django Reinhardt, a self-taught guitar maestro, and Dave Brubeck, who overcame his initial reluctance to learn piano, demonstrate that unconventional paths can lead to greatness.

Improv masters, like toddlers learning language, develop abstract models and rely less on specific examples, fostering creativity and problem-solving skills.

Creativity, however, can be stifled by excessive household rules and constraints. Parents of creative children tend to express their feelings after their children's actions rather than imposing restrictions beforehand.

The journey to musical mastery is a complex and often unpredictable one, requiring a balance of guidance, freedom, and a nurturing environment that encourages exploration and experimentation.

Key Takeaways And Learning

1. In 17th-century Venice, instrumental music underwent a transformation with new instruments, the establishment of major and minor keys, and the rise of virtuosos.

2. Antonio Vivaldi became the master of the concerto, while the figlie del coro, an all-female choir, captivated audiences across Europe.

3. The figlie del coro were orphaned foundlings who received a comprehensive education, including music, at the Ospedale della Pietà.

4. The Pietà's music program was rigorous, with figlie learning various instruments and performing a range of vocal and instrumental combinations.

5. The figlie's musical excellence propelled composers to unprecedented heights, laying the groundwork for the modern orchestra.

6. Parents and the media often seek the secret to musical success, emphasizing early instrument selection and focused practice.

7. However, research suggests that the amount of lesson or practice time is not a reliable predictor of musical excellence.

8. The distribution of effort among several instruments is crucial, as more proficient students tend to have played multiple instruments.

9. Learning classical music is a golf-like endeavor that defies the traditional road to success.

10. Many renowned musicians, including jazz and classical guitar teacher Cecchini, pianist Dave Brubeck, and improv maestro Django Reinhardt, had unconventional learning experiences.

11. Improv masters learn like toddlers, first learning the sounds and then the formal rules, similar to language learning.

12. Creativity may be hindered by strict household rules and constraints.

13. Improvising is a slow process that helps musicians develop problem-solving skills and discover their own voice.

Questions To Think About

1. How has instrumental music evolved since the 17th century?

_____

_____

_____

_____

_____

_____

_____

2. What was the role of the figlie del coro in Venetian music?

_____

_____

_____

_____

_____

_____

_____

3. How did the ospedali contribute to the development of musical talent?

_____

_____

_____

_____

_____

_____

_____

4. What is the significance of multi-instrument experience for musicians?

---

5. How does the Tiger Mother's approach to musical education compare to other methods?

---

6. What are the key findings of Sloboda's research on musical growth?

_____

_____

7. How does the distribution of effort among several instruments affect musical excellence?

_____

_____

_____

_____

_____

_____

_____

8. What are some examples of successful musicians who did not follow the traditional path to success?

_____

_____

_____

_____

_____

_____

_____

9. How do improv masters learn music?

_____

_____

_____

_____

_____

_____

_____

10. What is the Suzuki Method of music education, and how does it mirror natural language acquisition?

_____

_____

_____

_____

_____

_____

11. How can parents foster creativity in their children?

_____

_____

_____

_____

_____

_____

12. What is the importance of problem-solving skills for musicians?

_____

_____

_____

_____

_____

_____

_____

Personal Growth Activities

1. Explore A Variety Of Instruments:

• *Action:*

Encourage children to experiment with different instruments before specializing in one.

• *Exercise:*

Visit a music store or attend a music education event where children can try out various instruments. Discuss the different sounds, feels, and techniques required for each instrument.

2. Focus On Multi-Instrumentalism:

● *Action:*

Promote the learning of multiple instruments, even if a child shows early proficiency in one.

● *Exercise:*

Create a practice schedule that includes time for different instruments. Encourage children to explore different genres and styles of music on each instrument.

3. *Teach Improvisation And Problem-Solving:*

● *Action:*

Incorporate improvisation and problem-solving exercises into music lessons.

● *Exercise:*

Have children compose short melodies or rhythms on the spot. Encourage them to experiment with different combinations of notes, chords, and rhythms. Provide opportunities for children to perform their improvisations in front of an audience.

4. *Create A Supportive And Encouraging Environment:*

● *Action:*

Foster a supportive and encouraging environment for musical exploration and experimentation.

● *Exercise:*

Provide positive feedback and encouragement to children as they learn and grow musically. Avoid criticism or comparison to others. Encourage children to express their own musical ideas and styles.

5. Encourage Curiosity And Exploration:

• *Action:*

Encourage children to explore different genres of music and musical cultures.

• *Exercise:*

Attend concerts, music festivals, and cultural events together. Encourage children to listen to different types of music and discuss their thoughts and feelings about it.

6. Limit Household Rules And Prior Constraints:

• *Action:*

Review household rules and prior constraints that may be stifling creativity.

• *Exercise:*

Discuss with family members the importance of allowing children to explore and experiment freely. Encourage open communication and expression of ideas.

7. Provide Opportunities For Performance:

• *Action:*

Create opportunities for children to perform their music in front of an audience.

• *Exercise:*

Organize recitals, open mic nights, or talent shows where children can share their musical talents with others. Encourage children to perform in different settings and for different audiences.

Motivation

"The path to success is not always a straight line. Sometimes, it's a winding road, filled with unexpected twists and turns. But if you keep moving forward, you'll eventually reach your destination."

CHAPTER 4

***

Chapter Summary

Rethinking Math Education: Embracing Struggle For Long-Term Learning

TRADITIONAL MATH TEACHING methods, focused on rote memorization and excessive hint-giving, hinder students' long-term learning and adaptability. This approach fails to foster critical thinking and problem-solving skills necessary for success in higher education and the workforce.

Research indicates that desirable difficulties, such as spaced practice and self-testing, promote deeper understanding and retention. Struggling with problems initially may lead to slower progress, but it ultimately enhances learning outcomes.

Effective math teaching should prioritize "making connections" questions that encourage students to apply mathematical concepts to real-world scenarios and make abstract generalizations. Interleaving, or mixing different types of problems, also enhances inductive reasoning and the ability to transfer knowledge to novel situations.

However, students often resist desirable difficulties and prefer strategies that yield immediate results, even if they don't lead to lasting understanding. This highlights the need for teachers to adopt long-term perspectives and resist the temptation to provide excessive hints or simplify problems.

Moreover, education programs should emphasize "open" skills that can be applied to a wide range of problems, rather than "closed" skills that are specific to particular contexts. This approach promotes far transfer, or the ability to apply knowledge to new and unfamiliar situations.

In conclusion, effective math education should embrace struggle and desirable difficulties to cultivate adaptable and resilient learners. This requires a shift in mindset for both teachers and students, prioritizing long-term learning outcomes over immediate performance.

Key Takeaways And Learning

1. Students often struggle to relate the abstraction of a variable to more than one specific number in any given scenario.

2. Teachers frequently employ two types of questions: "using procedures" and "making connections" inquiries.

3. Making-connections challenges help students develop a deeper understanding of mathematical concepts, but they can also be difficult for students to solve.

4. Procedure practice is important in math, but when it takes up the entire math training plan, it can be problematic.

5. Desirable difficulties, such as the "generation effect," make learning more difficult and slower in the near term but more beneficial in the long run.

6. Excessive hint-giving in math classes stifles progress in the long run.

7. Spacing between practice sessions is critical for effective learning.

8. The Air Force Academy study showed that teachers who encouraged short-term hardship but long-term benefits did not benefit their students in the long run.

9. Students were selectively punishing teachers who provided them with the highest long-term benefits.

10. Interleaving, or diversified practice, is a learning strategy that enhances inductive reasoning by giving a variety of examples simultaneously.

11. Interleaving might deceive students about their own development.

12. Desirable problems in early childhood education programs might slow down learning and performance since they teach "closed" abilities that can be swiftly learned through repetition.

13. Programs should emphasize on "open" abilities that may be applied to new issues, such as "far transfer," in order to provide long-term academic benefits.

Questions To Think About

1. How can teachers help students understand the relevance of algebraic expressions in real-world scenarios?

_____

_____

_____

_____

_____

_____

_____

2. What are the differences in teaching methods used in different countries, and how do these methods impact student learning?

_____

_____

_____

_____

_____

_____

_____

3. Why is it important to balance procedure practice with making-connections questions in mathematics education?

_____

_____

_____

_____

_____

_____

_____

4. How does the "generation effect" promote long-term learning, and how can teachers incorporate it into their teaching strategies?

_____

_____

_____

_____

_____

_____

_____

5. What is the role of spacing and scattered practice in effective learning, and how can teachers implement these techniques in their classrooms?

_____

_____

_____

_____

_____

_____

_____

6. Why do students often punish teachers who provide them with the highest long-term benefits, and how can this be addressed?

_____

_____

_____

_____

_____

_____

_____

7. How has the shift in labor force demands impacted schools, and what teaching practices are necessary to meet these new requirements?

_____

_____

_____

_____

_____

_____

_____

8. How does interleaving enhance inductive reasoning and promote the application of knowledge to novel material?

_____

_____

_____

_____

_____

_____

9. Why might desirable problems in early childhood education programs slow down learning and performance, and how can programs be designed to

emphasize "open" abilities for long-term academic benefits?

_____

_____

_____

_____

_____

_____

_____

Personal Growth Activities

1. Encourage "Making Connections" Questions:

• *Action:*

Incorporate more "making connections" questions into your math lessons. These questions encourage students to think critically and apply their knowledge to real-world scenarios.

• *Exercise:*

Create a list of "making connections" questions related to the current math topic. Ask these questions during class discussions, group work, or individual assignments.

• *Analysis:*

Observe how students respond to these questions. Do they struggle to make connections? Do they come up with creative and insightful answers? Use this information to adjust your teaching approach and provide additional support as needed.

2. Implement "Spacing" Or Scattered Practice:

• *Action:*

Introduce "spacing" or scattered practice into your math lessons. Space out practice sessions over time, rather than cramming everything into a single session.

• *Exercise:*

Divide a math concept into smaller units or subtopics. Create a practice schedule that distributes these units over several days or weeks. This allows students to revisit the material multiple times, reinforcing their understanding and improving long-term retention.

• *Analysis:*

Monitor students' progress and assess their understanding of the material. Are they able to apply their knowledge to new problems and situations? Are they able to retain the information over time? Adjust your practice schedule accordingly.

3. Incorporate "Interleaving" Or Varied Practice:

• *Action:*

Use "interleaving" or varied practice to enhance students' inductive reasoning and problem-solving skills. Present different types of problems or examples simultaneously, rather than focusing on one type at a time.

• *Exercise:*

Create a set of math problems that cover a variety of concepts and skills. Mix up the order of the problems so that students have to apply different strategies and approaches.

• *Analysis:*

Observe how students respond to this type of practice. Do they struggle to switch between different problem types? Do they demonstrate flexibility and adaptability in their thinking? Use this information to adjust your teaching approach and provide additional support as needed.

Motivation

"Desirable difficulties, such as the 'generation effect,' make learning more difficult and slower in the near term but more beneficial in the long run."

CHAPTER 5

***

Chapter Summary

Unleashing The Power Of Analogical Thinking

IN THE 17TH century, Johannes Kepler revolutionized astronomy by questioning conventional beliefs and employing analogical thinking. He recognized that distant planets moved slower, leading him to develop the laws of planetary motion and establish astrophysics.

Analogical thinking involves identifying conceptual parallels across different domains or situations. It allows us to reason through unfamiliar problems and comprehend abstract concepts. Dedre Gentner, a leading expert in analogical thinking, highlights its importance in human cognition and creativity.

A classic example in cognitive psychology is Karl Duncker's hypothetical dilemma of a doctor needing to destroy a stomach tumor using rays. Analogies from other fields, such as a military strategy to capture a citadel, can inspire innovative solutions.

Research shows that our intuition often fails us when faced with ill-defined problems. We tend to rely on our experience-based instincts, which are well-suited for familiar situations. However, analogical thinking can help us overcome this limitation by drawing connections to seemingly unrelated problems.

In various fields, from venture capital to film industry, analogical thinking has been used to make accurate predictions and improve outcomes. Experiments have demonstrated that providing multiple analogies can stimulate idea generation and lead to more effective solutions.

Kepler's quest to redesign the universe began with a school assignment gone awry. His ability to draw analogies from unexpected sources, such as boats, brooms, and magnets, transformed astronomy. Today's world-class research facilities often foster an environment where unexpected discoveries serve as opportunities for breakthroughs.

Analogical thinking is a powerful tool that enables us to learn from diverse perspectives and solve complex problems. It challenges us to look beyond the immediate context and identify underlying structural similarities. By embracing analogical thinking, we can unlock new insights and drive innovation across various fields.

Key Takeaways And Learning

1. Kepler's deep analogical thinking led him to develop the laws of planetary motion and invent astrophysics.

2. Analogical thinking allows humans to reason through problems they have never encountered before.

3. The ability to think relationally is one of the reasons humans are dominating the world.

4. Analogies can help people solve problems by drawing on similarities between different situations.

5. Problem solving can be enhanced by drawing on analogies from other fields.

6. Our experience-based instincts are well-suited for problems that are repeated, but not for ill-defined challenges.

7. Focusing on a project's intricacies can lead to an overestimation of its success.

8. Analogical thinking can be used to accurately predict the success of movies and other projects.

9. Providing people with multiple analogies can help them generate more solutions to problems.

10. The more distant the analogy, the more effective it can be for idea production.

11. World-class research facilities often use analogies to push forward their research.

12. Scientists from different professional backgrounds can learn from each other by drawing comparisons to unexpected findings.

13. Analogical thinking can be taught, but it may require giving up a head start on a major or career.

14. Slowly acquired information, such as the ability to make connections, is sometimes disregarded in favor of an early start and specialization.

Questions To Think About

1. How can analogical thinking help us address complex problems?

_____

_____

_____

_____

_____

_____

_____

2. What are some examples of how analogical thinking has been used to solve problems in different fields?

_____

_____

_____

_____

_____

_____

_____

3. How can we overcome the natural tendency to take an "inside view" of a problem and instead focus on the "outside view"?

_____

_____

_____

_____

_____

_____

_____

4. How can analogical thinking be used to improve decision-making and forecasting?

_____

_____

_____

_____

_____

_____

_____

5. What are some challenges associated with using analogical thinking, and how can we address them?

_____

_____

_____

_____

_____

_____

_____

6. How can we foster analogical thinking in education and research environments?

_____

_____

_____

_____

_____

_____

_____

7. What are some real-world examples of how analogical thinking has led to breakthroughs and discoveries?

_____

_____

_____

_____

_____

_____

_____

8. How can we balance the benefits of analogical thinking with the need for specialization and expertise in different fields?

_____

_____

_____

_____

_____

_____

_____

Personal Growth Activities

1. Analogical Thinking Exercise:

• *Action:*

Practice analogical thinking by identifying similarities and differences between seemingly unrelated concepts.

• *Exercise:*

Choose a challenging problem or situation you're facing. Then, brainstorm a list of analogies that might provide insights or solutions. For example, if you're trying to improve your public speaking skills, you might think of analogies like "giving a speech is like performing on stage" or "convincing an audience is like winning over a jury."

• *Analysis:*

Reflect on the analogies you generated and consider how they might help you approach the problem or situation differently.

2. Outside View Perspective Exercise:

• *Action:*

Shift your perspective to the "outside view" by looking for underlying structural connections between different problems.

• *Exercise:*

Choose a problem or challenge you're facing and try to identify other situations or domains where similar structural patterns might exist. For example, if you're struggling with a conflict at work, you might think of analogies like "resolving a workplace conflict is like negotiating a peace treaty" or "mediating a dispute between friends."

• *Analysis:*

Explore the implications of the analogies you identified and consider how they might inform your approach to the problem or challenge.

3. Analogies For Problem Solving:

• *Action:*

Use analogies to generate creative solutions to problems.

• *Exercise:*

Choose a problem or challenge you're facing and brainstorm a list of analogies that might suggest potential solutions. For example, if you're trying to increase sales for your business, you might think of analogies like "growing a business is like cultivating a garden" or "attracting customers is like fishing."

• *Analysis:*

Evaluate the analogies you generated and consider how they might inspire new ideas or approaches to solving the problem or challenge.

Motivation

"Our ability to think relationally is one of the reasons we are dominating the world."

CHAPTER 6

✱✱✱

Chapter Summary

Vincent Van Gogh: A Journey Through Art And Self-Discovery

VINCENT VAN GOGH, a Dutch post-impressionist painter, embarked on a remarkable artistic journey marked by struggles, perseverance, and a profound impact on the art world.

Early Life And Artistic Development:

• Born into a creative family, van Gogh's early life was shaped by his mother's love for music and art.

• Despite his initial lack of artistic skills, he pursued art education and worked at an art dealership.

- A series of setbacks, including social struggles and academic difficulties, led him to become a missionary in South America.

Return To Art And Unique Style:

- Encouraged by his family, van Gogh returned to art and enrolled in an art school, where he embraced a bold and expressive style.

- He experimented with various techniques, including watercolors and oil paints, constantly pushing the boundaries of artistic expression.

Artistic Legacy And Impact:

- Van Gogh's work, characterized by vibrant colors, bold brushstrokes, and emotional intensity, ushered in a new era of art.

- His paintings challenged traditional notions of beauty and paved the way for contemporary art.

- His influence extended beyond his lifetime, inspiring generations of artists and shaping the course of modern art.

The Value Of Quitting And Embracing New Paths:

• Research suggests that quitting can lead to improved outcomes in various aspects of life, including career and personal growth.

• Successful individuals often demonstrate the courage to abandon unproductive paths and pursue better-suited endeavors.

• Embracing failure and learning from setbacks can lead to greater success and fulfillment in the long run.

Grit, Passion, And The Pursuit Of Success:

• Psychological factors such as grit, passion, and work ethic play a significant role in determining success.

• Individuals with high levels of grit are more likely to persist in the face of challenges and achieve their goals.

• Passion and dedication are essential drivers of success, propelling individuals to overcome obstacles and excel in their chosen fields.

The Sunk Cost Fallacy And The Courage To Change:

• The sunk cost fallacy often prevents individuals from abandoning unproductive endeavors, even when it is clear that they are not a good fit.

• Overcoming this fallacy requires recognizing when to quit and embracing new opportunities that better align with one's skills and interests.

• Changing paths can lead to increased engagement, satisfaction, and overall success.

Embracing Change And Finding The Right Fit:

• Finding the right match between one's skills, interests, and career aspirations is crucial for long-term success and fulfillment.

• Being open to change, exploring new possibilities, and pursuing passions can lead to a more fulfilling and rewarding life.

• Embracing change and seeking the right fit allows individuals to maximize their potential and achieve their full potential.

Key Takeaways And Learning

1. Early and late specializers in the job market often have better matches.

2. Switching careers can lead to improved growth rates and enjoyment as professionals use their experience to find better matches.

3. Informed switching can boost student performance after teachers switch schools, and this benefit is not caused by higher-achieving schools or better students.

4. Psychological factors such as grit and work ethic can aid in predicting quit rates.

5. Grit, or consistency of interests, can predict a person's tenacity in a competitive field.

6. Understanding when to quit is a strategic advantage, and everyone should list the circumstances under which they should quit.

7. Passion and perseverance are necessary for success in many areas of life, including sports and employment.

8. The sunk cost fallacy states that humans are hesitant to abandon anything in which they have committed time or money, even if it is no longer available.

9. Changing your passion or emphasis can increase your chances of finding the right match.

Questions To Think About

1. How has your personal experience influenced your career choices?

_____

_____

_____

_____

_____

_____

_____

2. What are your strengths and weaknesses, and how have they shaped your career path?

_____

_____

_____

_____

_____

_____

_____

3. What are your long-term career goals, and how do they align with your current skills and interests?

_____

_____

_____

_____

_____

_____

_____

4. How do you stay motivated and focused on your career goals?

_____

_____

_____

_____

_____

_____

_____

5. What challenges have you faced in your career, and how have you overcome them?

_____

_____

_____

_____

_____

_____

_____

6. What advice would you give to someone who is just starting out in their career?

_____

_____

_____

_____

_____

_____

_____

7. How do you manage your time and prioritize your tasks?

_____

_____

_____

_____

_____

_____

8. How do you stay up-to-date on industry trends and developments?

_____

_____

_____

_____

_____

_____

_____

9. How do you network with other professionals in your field?

_____

_____

_____

_____

_____

_____

_____

10. How do you handle stress and pressure in your career?

_____

_____

_____

_____

_____

Personal Growth Activities

1. Self-Reflection:

• *Action:*

Take some time to reflect on your own educational and career journey. Identify moments when you switched paths or made significant changes.

• *Exercise:*

Create a timeline of your life, marking key decisions and changes. For each decision, write a brief explanation of why you made the change and what the outcome was.

• *Analysis:*

Look for patterns or themes in your decision-making. Did you tend to switch paths based on external factors (e.g., job market conditions) or internal factors (e.g., personal interests or values)? Did you experience any sunk cost fallacies or regrets?

2. Swot Analysis:

• *Action:*

Conduct a SWOT analysis of your current situation. Identify your strengths, weaknesses, opportunities, and threats.

• *Exercise:*

Write down a list of your skills, talents, and interests. Then, list any areas where you feel you need improvement. Consider your current job market and any potential opportunities or challenges.

• *Analysis:*

Use your SWOT analysis to identify areas where you might benefit from a change. Consider whether your current path aligns with your strengths and interests. Are there any opportunities that you're missing out on? Are there any threats that you need to address?

3. Career Exploration:

• *Action:*

Explore different career options and industries. Research different jobs, talk to people who work in those fields, and learn about the skills and education required.

• *Exercise:*

Attend career fairs, informational interviews, and networking events. Take online career assessments or quizzes to help you identify potential career paths.

• *Analysis:*

Keep an open mind and be willing to consider different possibilities. Don't be afraid to step outside of your comfort zone and try something new. Consider your values, interests, and long-term goals when making career decisions.

Motivation

"Winners quit fast when they see that something isn't working." • Seth Godin

CHAPTER 7

***

Chapter Summary

Unconventional Paths To Success: Embracing Uncertainty And Adaptability

FRANCES HESSELBEIN'S REMARKABLE leadership journey highlights the value of adaptability and embracing unconventional paths. Despite facing discrimination, she rose to prominence through her unwavering commitment to inclusivity and community service. Her leadership at the Girl Scouts and subsequent restructuring of the organization exemplify her visionary and transformative abilities.

Research reveals that many successful individuals, including Charles Darwin and Nike co-founder Phil Knight, navigated circuitous career paths, often driven by short-term planning and a willingness to explore new opportunities. The "standardisation covenant," which emphasizes early specialization and stability, may limit the potential for personal growth and adaptability.

The "marshmallow test," while widely recognized, has been criticized for its simplistic interpretation. Personality traits are influenced by both nature and nurture, and individuals' preferences, values, and personalities evolve over time. This fluidity challenges the notion of setting long-term goals based on early childhood assessments.

Herminia Ibarra's research emphasizes the importance of experiential learning and self-discovery. She suggests that individuals can improve their career satisfaction by sampling various activities, social groups, and jobs, and by reflecting on their experiences to refine their personal narratives. Conventional wisdom often promotes a linear path to success, but Ibarra advocates for a more exploratory and iterative approach.

Paul Graham and other successful individuals exemplify the benefits of embracing uncertainty and pursuing promising opportunities. They challenge the "plan-and-implement" methodology, which assumes a fixed long-term plan. Instead, they advocate for ongoing experimentation, networking, and seeking mentorship to uncover new possibilities.

Chrissie Wellington, Ciarán Hinds, and other remarkable individuals found success later in life by following their passions and embracing unconventional paths. Outsider artists, often self-taught and initially unrecognized, have gained recognition for their unique perspectives and artistic expression.

The stories of these individuals underscore the importance of adaptability, resilience, and the willingness to embrace uncertainty. Embracing a non-linear career path allows for ongoing learning, personal growth, and the discovery of unexpected opportunities.

Key Takeaways And Learning

Key Points and Lessons:

1. Frances Hesselbein's leadership journey emphasizes the value of inclusivity, resourcefulness, collaborative leadership, and finding common ground.

2. Unorthodox and circuitous professional paths are common, and short-term planning often leads to success.

3. The "standardisation covenant" promotes stability but may hinder self-discovery and growth.

4. Personality and preferences evolve over time, making long-term goal-setting challenging.

5. The "marshmallow test" highlights the importance of self-control but should not be overinterpreted.

6. Our "story of me" expands as we live and experience new things.

7. We learn who we are through our experiences, not before.

8. Sampling activities, social groups, and jobs helps us improve match quality throughout life.

9. Drastic career changes can lead to fulfillment and personal growth.

10. Short-term planning and experimentation are valuable strategies for career exploration.

11. Successful individuals often build their careers from promising beginnings, rather than following a rigid plan.

12. Passion and experimentation can lead to unexpected career paths and achievements.

13. Outsider art and self-taught artists challenge traditional talent development programs and offer unique perspectives.

Questions To Think About

1. What were the key factors that influenced Frances Hesselbein's leadership style and career trajectory?

_____

_____

_____

_____

_____

_____

2. How did Hesselbein's experiences in her early life shape her values and approach to leadership?

_____

_____

_____

_____

_____

_____

_____

3. What are some of the challenges and opportunities that leaders face when trying to create inclusive and diverse organizations?

_____

_____

_____

_____

_____

_____

_____

4. What are some of the ways in which individuals can develop their leadership skills and capabilities?

_____

_____

_____

_____

_____

_____

_____

5. How can leaders effectively navigate the challenges and opportunities of leading in a rapidly changing and uncertain environment?

_____

_____

_____

_____

_____

_____

_____

6. What are some of the common misconceptions or myths about leadership that individuals and organizations should be aware of?

_____

_____

_____

_____

_____

_____

_____

7. How can leaders create a culture of innovation and creativity within their organizations?

_____

_____

_____

_____

_____

_____

_____

8. What are some of the key trends and developments in the field of leadership that individuals and organizations should be aware of?

_____

_____

_____

_____

_____

_____

_____

9. How can leaders effectively balance the need for short-term results with the need for long-term sustainability and success?

_____

_____

_____

_____

_____

_____

_____

10. What are some of the key lessons that can be learned from the experiences of successful leaders across different fields and industries?

_____

_____

_____

_____

_____

_____

_____

Personal Growth Activities

1. Embrace The Circuitous Path:

• *Action:*

Reflect on your own career journey. Have you taken a linear or a more winding path?

• *Exercise:*

Create a timeline of your professional experiences, including jobs, volunteer work, and personal projects. Identify key turning points and moments of growth.

• *Analysis:*

Embrace the twists and turns in your career path. Recognize that unconventional journeys can lead to unique opportunities and valuable lessons.

2. Experiment And Sample:

• *Action:*

Step outside your comfort zone and try new activities, hobbies, or career paths.

• *Exercise:*

Make a list of activities or industries you're curious about. Set aside time to explore them through books, online courses, or hands-on experiences.

• *Analysis:*

Pay attention to what sparks your interest and what doesn't. Reflect on how these experiences contribute to your evolving sense of self and career goals.

3. Short-Term Planning And Rapid Experimentation:

• *Action:*

Adopt a short-term planning approach. Set smaller, achievable goals and focus on the immediate steps you can take to move forward.

• *Exercise:*

Break down your long-term goals into smaller, more manageable steps. Set deadlines for each step and track your progress.

• *Analysis:*

Celebrate your accomplishments along the way and adjust your plan as needed. Embrace the idea of being your own scientist, conducting experiments and learning from the results.

Motivation

"The best way to predict your future is to create it."

CHAPTER 8

***

Chapter Summary

Outsider Advantage: Unconventional Solutions To Complex Problems

DR. ALPHONSE BINGHAM, a chemist at Eli Lilly, recognized that innovative solutions often lie beyond traditional boundaries. He founded InnoCentive, a platform that connects companies with "solvers" outside their fields of expertise to tackle challenging problems. Over a third of InnoCentive's challenges were successfully solved, demonstrating the effectiveness of this "outsider advantage."

Critics initially dismissed the contributions of outsiders, but numerous examples showcase their remarkable achievements. For instance, Bruce Cragin, a retired engineer, solved a 30-year-old NASA problem by utilizing radio waves detected by telescopes. John Davis, a chemist, devised a solution to the oil spill problem inspired by his experience with concrete vibrators.

InnoCentive's success highlights the value of seeking solutions from diverse perspectives. Kaggle, a platform for presenting machine-learning problems, has also capitalized on this trend, recognizing the potential of multidisciplinary problem-solving.

Specialization, while valuable, can limit creative problem-solving. Jill Viles, a muscular dystrophy patient, shared a genetic mutation with Olympic sprinter Priscilla Lopes-Schliep. Jill's observation led to a genetic test for Priscilla, potentially helping others with muscular dystrophy develop stronger muscles.

Jill's story further illustrates the power of outsider perspectives. She identified a genetic link between herself and Priscilla, leading to the discovery of a new disease-causing mutation. This breakthrough highlights the importance of recognizing genetic differences in athletes and the potential of genetic testing in diagnosing hereditary diseases.

Jill and Priscilla's collaboration also led to the discovery of a new subtype of partial lipodystrophy, known as Dunnigan type. This finding prompted research into the protein SREBP1, which may play a role in muscle and fat loss.

InnoCentive and similar platforms demonstrate the value of enlisting outsiders to solve problems. By tapping into diverse perspectives, organizations can overcome challenges that may have stumped experts within their own ranks.

Key Takeaways And Learning

1. Outsiders and non-experts can often provide valuable insights and solutions to problems that have stumped experts.

2. The "outsider advantage" concept involves seeking solutions from individuals with diverse backgrounds and experiences.

3. InnoCentive is a platform that allows companies to post challenges and prizes for outside solvers to address.

4. Examples of successful outside-in solvers include Bruce Cragin, who solved a NASA problem using radio waves, and John Davis, who developed a method to remove cold chocolate mousse from rescue barges.

5. Increased specialization within organizations can limit creative problem solving and open up opportunities for outsiders.

6. Platforms like Kaggle allow for the presentation of machine learning problems to a wide range of solvers.

7. Interdisciplinary problem solving can lead to innovative solutions, as demonstrated by Don Swanson's work in information science.

8. Jill Viles, a muscular dystrophy patient, identified a genetic mutation shared with Olympic sprinter Priscilla Lopes-Schliep, leading to research into the development of muscles closer to the Priscilla end of the human body continuum.

9. Genetic testing can aid in the diagnosis of hereditary illnesses, as seen in the case of Jill and her father's heart troubles.

10. Recognizing genetic differences in athletes can help in understanding their performance and potential.

11. Jill and Priscilla's shared subtype of partial lipodystrophy, Dunnigan type, led to the discovery of a genetic link between their conditions.

12. The work of French researcher Etienne Lefai on the protein SREBP1 may provide insights into the regulation of muscle and fat loss in individuals with lipodystrophy.

13. InnoCentive provides a platform for nonspecialists to contribute to the advancement of genetic illnesses.

Questions To Think About

1. What is the "outsider advantage" concept, and how has it been applied to different disciplines?

_____

_____

_____

_____

_____

_____

_____

2. How does InnoCentive help organizations solve problems using outside-in solvers?

_____

_____

_____

_____

_____

_____

_____

3. Provide examples of individuals who have successfully solved problems using the outsider advantage.

4. What are the challenges and limitations of relying solely on specialists to solve problems?

_____

_____

_____

_____

_____

_____

_____

5. How can organizations encourage and leverage the contributions of outsiders in problem-solving?

_____

_____

_____

_____

_____

_____

_____

6. What is the importance of recognizing genetic differences in athletes, and how can genetic testing contribute to diagnosing hereditary illnesses?

_____
_____
_____
_____
_____
_____

_____

7. Discuss the significance of the discovery that Jill and Priscilla shared the same subtype of lipodystrophy and how it led to a life-changing medical operation.

8. How can platforms like InnoCentive contribute to the advancement of genetic illnesses by involving nonspecialists?

_____
_____
_____
_____
_____
_____

_____

Personal Growth Activities

1. Identify And Frame Challenges:

• *Action:*

Identify problems or challenges within your organization that could benefit from a fresh perspective. Frame these challenges in a way that appeals to a diverse range of potential solvers.

• *Exercise:*

Brainstorm with colleagues from different departments or industries to identify challenges that might be solved by outsiders. Craft a clear and concise challenge statement that highlights the problem, the desired outcome, and any relevant constraints.

• *Analysis:*

Evaluate the challenge statement to ensure it is specific, measurable, achievable, relevant, and time-bound (SMART).

2. Engage Outsiders And Dilettantes:

• *Action:*

Seek out and engage individuals with diverse backgrounds, expertise, and perspectives who may have unique insights into your challenge. This could include people from different industries, academia, or even hobbyists with relevant knowledge.

• *Exercise:*

Collaborate with external partners, such as universities, research institutions, or online platforms like Kaggle, to connect with potential solvers. Host workshops or challenges to attract creative solutions from a variety of sources.

• *Analysis:*

Assess the diversity of perspectives and expertise among your solvers. Consider how their unique backgrounds and experiences might contribute to innovative solutions.

3. Foster A Culture Of Openness And Collaboration:

• *Action:*

Create an organizational culture that values and encourages outside-in thinking. Promote collaboration and knowledge sharing across departments and disciplines.

• *Exercise:*

Implement mechanisms for soliciting ideas and feedback from employees, customers, and external stakeholders. Encourage employees to actively seek out and incorporate diverse perspectives into their work.

• *Analysis:*

Evaluate the effectiveness of your organization's culture in fostering outside-in thinking. Measure the impact of external collaborations on problem-solving and innovation.

Additional Tips:

• *Clearly Define Roles And Responsibilities:*

Ensure that outsiders and internal stakeholders have a clear understanding of their roles, responsibilities, and expected contributions.

• *Provide The Necessary Resources:*

Equip outsiders with the necessary resources, data, and support to effectively contribute to the problem-solving process.

• *Maintain Open Communication:*

Foster open communication channels between outsiders and internal stakeholders to facilitate effective collaboration and feedback.

• *Evaluate And Reward Success:*

Recognize and reward successful contributions from outsiders. This can encourage continued participation and engagement.

Motivation

"Think outside the box and embrace the power of unconventional ideas. Sometimes, the key to solving a problem lies not in specialized knowledge, but in a fresh perspective and an open mind."

CHAPTER 9

***

Chapter Summary

Lateral Thinking And Polymathic Innovation: Lessons From Nintendo And 3M

Key Points:

• *Nintendo'S Success:*

Gunpei Yokoi's "lateral thinking with withered technology" approach led to innovations like the Game & Watch and Game Boy, which revolutionized the gaming industry.

• *Polymathic Innovators:*

Generalist inventors with diverse backgrounds often make significant contributions, as they can connect seemingly unrelated ideas and fields.

• *Balancing Specialization And Breadth:*

While specialization is important, breadth of experience and knowledge can be crucial for innovation in uncertain environments.

• *Importance Of Communication:*

Serial innovators need to effectively communicate with experts from different fields to integrate diverse information and create novel solutions.

Case Study: Nintendo'S Innovation

• Gunpei Yokoi, a key figure at Nintendo, emphasized "lateral thinking" and repurposing existing technology to create new products.

• The Game & Watch and Game Boy were hugely successful due to their affordability, portability, and innovative design.

• Yokoi's approach encouraged young engineers to explore new applications for technology beyond their specific expertise.

Case Study: 3M'S Multilayer Optical Material

• A team led by John Ouderkirk developed a multilayer optical material with wide applications, from cell phones to solar panels.

• The success of this invention was attributed not only to technical expertise but also to the team's diverse backgrounds and ability to see "adjacent possibilities."

• Generalist inventors with a broad range of experience made significant contributions to the project.

Implications For Innovation And Talent Management

• Organizations should value and seek out individuals with diverse interests and backgrounds, as they often possess the creativity and adaptability needed for innovation.

• Hiring managers should look beyond hyperspecialization and consider candidates with a variety of experiences and skills.

• In uncertain environments, broad experience and the ability to integrate diverse information are invaluable assets.

- Serial innovators often thrive in complex and ambiguous situations, demonstrating systems thinking and the ability to communicate across disciplines.

Conclusion:

Lateral thinking, polymathic innovation, and a diverse workforce are key factors driving innovation in today's rapidly changing world. Organizations that embrace these principles and foster a culture of exploration and experimentation are more likely to succeed in the face of uncertainty and disruption.

Key Takeaways And Learning

1. Kenichi Yokoi, founder of Nintendo, was a pioneer in the game industry known for his unique console designs.

2. The Wii console, despite criticism, was seen by Yokoi as an empowering breakthrough that introduced video games to a new audience.

3. Yokoi's greatest failure came when he deviated from his design principles, such as with the Virtual Boy gaming headgear.

4. Yokoi believed that lateral and vertical thinkers worked best together, even in highly technical sectors.

5. Physicist Freeman Dyson emphasized the importance of dedicated and imaginative "birds" in the scientific community.

6. A team led by John Ouderkirk created an optical material that can almost flawlessly reflect light, impacting various industries.

7. Ouderkirk and his team discovered that an invention's success depends not only on technical specialization but also on "adjacent stuff."

8. Generalist inventors who have worked in numerous disciplines often produce the most significant contributions.

9. Polymaths, with depth in a core field but not as much as specialists, tend to thrive in organizations and receive recognition.

10. Breadth of experience is critical to success in the IT business, as teams with diverse technologies are more likely to make a splash.

11. Individual innovators with broad experience can outperform teams in terms of innovation.

12. Teams of specialists operate well in similar circumstances, while serial innovators excel in unknown and ambiguous situations.

13. Human resource managers should value diverse interests and experiences in potential hires, especially for complex and challenging roles.

Questions To Think About

1. How can lateral thinking with withered technology help you find new applications for old technology?

_____

_____

_____

_____

_____

_____

_____

2. How can the Unusual (or Alternative) Uses Task help you think more creatively?

_____

_____

_____

_____

_____

_____

_____

3. What are the advantages of being a generalist inventor?

_____

_____

_____

_____

_____

_____

_____

4. How can you increase your breadth of experience and become a more T-shaped person?

_____

_____

_____

_____

_____

_____

_____

5. How can teams of specialists and teams with diverse technologies work together to achieve success?

_____

_____

_____

_____

_____

_____

_____

6. What are the characteristics of serial innovators?

_____

_____

_____

_____

_____

_____

_____

7. How can human resource managers identify and hire serial innovators?

_____

_____

_____

_____

_____

_____

_____

8. In what situations is broad experience more valuable than limited specialization?

_____

_____

_____

_____

_____

_____

_____

Personal Growth Activities

1. Identify Your Polymathic Potential:

• *Action:*

Evaluate your skillset and interests. Do you possess depth in a core field but also have a wide range of knowledge and experience in other areas? Do you enjoy learning and exploring new subjects?

• *Exercise:*

Create a skills inventory that includes not only your technical expertise but also your soft skills, hobbies, and personal interests. Identify areas where you have depth and areas where you would like to expand your knowledge.

• *Analysis:*

Assess your potential for becoming a polymath. Consider how your diverse skills and interests might intersect and lead to innovative ideas.

2. Embrace Lateral Thinking:

• *Action:*

Practice thinking outside the box and challenging conventional wisdom. Look for alternative solutions and unexpected connections between seemingly unrelated concepts.

• *Exercise:*

Engage in brainstorming sessions with diverse groups of people. Present a problem or challenge and encourage participants to come up with unconventional ideas.

• *Analysis:*

Evaluate the ideas generated during the brainstorming session. Were there any unexpected or groundbreaking solutions that emerged from the diverse perspectives?

3. Cultivate A Growth Mindset:

• *Action:*

Embrace challenges and setbacks as opportunities for learning and growth. Be open to acquiring new skills and expanding your knowledge base.

• *Exercise:*

Set goals for personal and professional development. Identify areas where you want to improve and take steps to acquire new skills or knowledge.

• *Analysis:*

Reflect on your progress toward your goals. Celebrate your achievements and learn from any setbacks. Recognize that continuous learning and growth are essential for staying relevant and innovative in a rapidly changing world.

Motivation

"Don't be afraid to think differently and challenge the status quo. Innovation often comes from unexpected places."

CHAPTER 10

***

Chapter Summary

The Pitfalls Of Dogmatic Predictions: Lessons From History

PAUL EHRLICH'S DIRE predictions of overpopulation and resource depletion in his 1968 book "The Population Bomb" sparked a debate with economist Julian Simon, who emphasized technological progress and innovation. While the global population has indeed grown, it is now slowing, highlighting the need for balanced perspectives.

Expert forecasts often fall short due to overconfidence and dogmatic adherence to their worldviews. Philip Tetlock's research revealed that experts frequently perform poorly in predicting outcomes, despite recognizing their own fallibility. This phenomenon is exacerbated when forecasts have a high likelihood of being published.

The collapse of the Soviet Union in 1991 serves as a cautionary tale. Experts who focused narrowly on specific factors (hedgehogs) were outperformed by those who considered a wider range of perspectives (foxes).

The Good Judgement Project demonstrated that diverse teams of forecasters can outperform individual experts, intelligence analysts, and prediction markets. Successful forecasters possess intelligence, numeracy, and a broad range of experiences, allowing them to integrate multiple perspectives and adapt their predictions as new information emerges.

Political polarization can lead to dogmatic thinking, making individuals resistant to evidence that contradicts their beliefs. Active open-mindedness and a willingness to seek out opposing viewpoints are essential for accurate forecasting.

Analogical reasoning and effective feedback loops can improve forecasting accuracy. Forecasters should focus on identifying structural similarities between seemingly unrelated events rather than relying solely on past experiences.

In conclusion, dogmatic predictions often fail to account for the complexity and interconnectedness of global systems. Successful forecasting requires a balanced approach, considering diverse perspectives, actively seeking out new information, and continuously refining mental models based on feedback.

Key Takeaways And Learning

1. Paul Ehrlich predicted a cataclysmic apocalypse caused by overpopulation, while Julian Simon emphasized the "green revolution" and technological achievements.

2. The world's population doubled between 1900 and 2008, despite erroneous forecasts of excessive population growth.

3. Philip Tetlock's research on expert forecasts during the Cold War found that experts often perform poorly in predicting.

4. Experts tend to be overconfident in their judgments and do not learn from their mistakes.

5. The Good Judgement Project showed that groups of diverse forecasters can make better predictions than individuals.

6. Good forecasters are intelligent, good with numbers, and have a broad range of knowledge.

7. The best forecasters are actively open-minded and willing to consider opposing viewpoints.

8. Politically diverse adults are more likely to be dogmatic about politically polarizing scientific topics.

9. Skilled forecasters use analogical reasoning and rely on intuition and rigorous feedback to improve their accuracy.

10. Learning involves putting experience aside and making adjustments to beliefs based on new information.

Questions To Think About

1. What are some of Paul Ehrlich's and Julian Simon's erroneous forecasts?

_____

_____

_____

_____

_____

_____

_____

2. How did the global population growth rate change from 1900 to 2008?

_____

_____

_____

_____

_____

_____

_____

3. What is the "green revolution"?

_____

_____

_____

_____

_____

_____

_____

4. What was the National Research Council committee on American-Soviet ties?

_____

_____

_____

_____

_____

_____

_____

5. What did Philip Tetlock's research on expert forecasts find?

_____

_____

_____

_____

_____

_____

_____

6. What is the Intelligence Advanced Research Projects Activity (IARPA)?

_____

_____

_____

_____

_____

_____

_____

7. What is the Good Judgement Project?

_____

_____

_____

_____

_____

_____

_____

8. What are some of the characteristics of good forecasters?

_____

_____

_____

_____

_____

_____

9. How can forecasters improve their accuracy?

_____

_____

_____

_____

_____

_____

10. What is "wicked learning"?

_____

_____

_____

_____

_____

_____

_____

11. How can forecasters foster a learning environment?

_____

_____

_____

_____

_____

_____

_____

Personal Growth Activities

1. Examining Expert Forecasts:

• *Action:*

Collect a set of expert predictions on a variety of topics (e.g., economic trends, political outcomes, scientific breakthroughs).

• *Exercise:*

Analyze the accuracy of these predictions over time. Were the experts generally correct, or did they make significant errors?

• *Analysis:*

Consider the factors that might influence the accuracy of expert forecasts. Were the experts too narrow in their focus (hedgehogs) or did they consider a wide range of perspectives (foxes)? Did they actively seek out evidence that challenged their assumptions?

2. Developing Active Open-Mindedness:

• *Action:*

Practice actively seeking out information that challenges your existing beliefs and assumptions.

• *Exercise:*

Choose a topic that you feel strongly about and make an effort to find evidence that contradicts your position. Read articles, watch documentaries, and talk to people who have different viewpoints.

• *Analysis:*

Reflect on how your beliefs and assumptions have changed as a result of this exercise. Did you become more open to new ideas? Did you find that your original position was strengthened?

3. Creating A Learning Environment:

• *Action:*

Establish a system for tracking your predictions and evaluating their accuracy over time.

• *Exercise:*

Keep a journal or spreadsheet where you record your predictions, along with the reasons behind them. When the outcomes are known, compare your predictions to the actual results.

• *Analysis:*

Identify areas where your predictions were accurate and areas where you made errors. What factors contributed to your successes and failures? How can you improve your forecasting skills in the future?

Motivation

"The greatest glory in living lies not in never falling, but in rising every time we fall." • Nelson Mandela

CHAPTER 11

***

Chapter Summary

Navigating Organizational Disasters: Lessons From Challenger, Wildland Fires, And The Pjs

ORGANIZATIONAL DECISION-MAKING IS often fraught with challenges, especially when faced with ambiguous or unprecedented situations. Case studies from the Challenger disaster, wildland fires, and the PJs in Afghanistan offer valuable lessons in navigating such crises.

1. The Perils Of Overreliance On Quantitative Analysis:

The Challenger disaster highlighted the dangers of relying solely on quantitative analysis. NASA's focus on numerical data led them to overlook crucial qualitative factors, resulting in the catastrophic failure of the space shuttle.

2. *Inflexible Adherence To Familiar Tools And Procedures:*

Both wildland firefighters and NASA engineers exhibited a tendency to stick to their familiar tools and procedures, even when circumstances demanded adaptation. This inflexibility contributed to tragic outcomes.

3. *The Importance Of Improvisation And Adaptability:*

In contrast, the PJs in Afghanistan demonstrated the value of improvisation and adaptability. They were willing to deviate from standard protocols to accommodate the unique challenges of their mission, ultimately leading to a successful rescue.

4. *Creating A Healthy Tension Between Formal And Informal Structures:*

Effective organizations strike a balance between formal procedures and informal individualism. This allows for both adherence to rules and the freedom to challenge conventional wisdom when necessary.

5. *The Power Of Diversity And Dissent:*

Diversity of perspectives and the willingness to dissent can enhance decision-making by exposing blind spots and challenging assumptions.

6. The Need For Healthy Conflict And Incongruence:

Incongruence, or the ability to hold seemingly contradictory ideas, can be beneficial in problem-solving. It encourages learning from experience and adaptation to new conditions.

7. The Role Of Leadership In Fostering A Culture Of Safety And Innovation:

Leaders play a crucial role in shaping an organizational culture that values safety, innovation, and adaptability. They must encourage open communication and a willingness to challenge the status quo.

8. The Importance Of Context-Specific Tools And Approaches:

The effectiveness of tools and approaches depends on the specific context. What works in one situation may not be suitable in another.

These lessons underscore the need for organizations to foster a culture of flexibility, adaptability, and diversity of thought. By encouraging healthy tension and a willingness to question established norms, organizations can better navigate complex and uncertain environments.

Key Takeaways And Learning

1. Relying too heavily on quantitative analysis can lead to overlooking critical qualitative factors, as in the case of the Challenger disaster.

2. Experienced professionals may revert to overlearned behaviors and tools that may not be appropriate in new or changing situations.

3. In high-pressure situations, individuals and teams may struggle to adapt and abandon familiar tools and strategies, even when necessary.

4. Effective leaders and organizations embrace a wide range of perspectives and approaches to problem-solving, avoiding the dangers of unthinking obedience and reckless divergence.

5. Incongruence in problem-solving can be beneficial, promoting learning from experience and adaptation to new conditions.

6. Creating a healthy tension within an organization, where individuals feel empowered to speak up and challenge the status quo, can lead to better decision-making and outcomes.

7. Focusing on specific tools and techniques without considering the broader context can lead to ineffective or harmful outcomes, as in the case of stent placement for stable chest discomfort.

8. Diversity in approaches and perspectives is essential for a healthy ecosystem and effective problem-solving.

Questions To Think About

1. What are the challenges and risks associated with relying too heavily on quantitative analysis?

_____
_____
_____
_____
_____
_____
_____

2. How can relying on overlearned behaviors lead to inflexibility and poor decision-making?

_____
_____
_____
_____
_____
_____
_____

3. How can NASA's Challenger disaster be interpreted as an example of the failure to adapt to new conditions?

_____
_____
_____
_____
_____
_____
_____

4. What lessons can be learned from the wildland firefighters' tragedy in Mann Gulch, where they refused to abandon their tools and lost their lives?

_____
_____
_____
_____
_____

_____

_____

5. How can organizations develop leaders who are knowledgeable about their tools but also willing to drop them when necessary?

_____

_____

_____

_____

_____

_____

_____

6. How can incongruence in problem-solving be advantageous for managers and organizations?

_____

_____

_____

_____

_____

_____

_____

7. How did William Lucas's transition from a compliance culture to a blend of formal procedural culture and

informal individualism impact NASA's culture and decision-making?

_____

_____

_____

_____

_____

_____

_____

8. How did Karl Weick's tools insight help interventional cardiologists and orthopaedic surgeons re-evaluate the effectiveness of their traditional methods?

_____

_____

_____

_____

_____

_____

9. How can organizations create a healthy ecosystem that promotes diversity and encourages different perspectives?

_____

_____

_____

_____

_____

_____

_____

10. How can organizations balance the risks of unthinking obedience and reckless divergence in decision-making?

_____

_____

_____

_____

_____

_____

_____

Personal Growth Activities

1. Assess Your Decision-Making Process:

• *Action:*

Reflect on your own decision-making process and identify situations where you might be relying too heavily on a particular tool or approach. Consider instances where you've stuck to a familiar method even when conditions changed.

• *Exercise:*

Describe a situation where you made a decision based on quantitative data. Analyze whether there were other relevant factors that you overlooked due to your focus on the data.

• *Analysis:*

Are there biases or limitations in your decision-making process that may lead you to overlook important information? Identify areas where you could benefit from considering a broader range of perspectives and tools.

2. Encourage Diverse Perspectives And Dissent:

• *Action:*

In group discussions or decision-making processes, actively seek out and encourage diverse opinions and perspectives. Create an environment where people feel comfortable challenging the status quo and expressing dissenting views.

• *Exercise:*

In a group setting, present a complex problem or challenge. Ask team members to share their initial thoughts and solutions. Then, facilitate a discussion where they can challenge each other's ideas and explore alternative approaches.

• *Analysis:*

Observe how the diversity of perspectives influences the quality of the discussion and the final decision. Reflect on how embracing incongruence can lead to more creative and effective solutions.

3. Embrace Incongruence And Adapt To Changing Conditions:

• *Action:*

Practice recognizing situations where your usual tools or approaches might not be the most effective. Be open to changing your strategy or seeking alternative solutions when circumstances demand it.

• *Exercise:*

Identify a task or project that you're currently working on. Consider different ways to approach it, even if they deviate from your usual methods. Experiment with different tools or strategies and see how they impact the outcome.

• *Analysis:*

Reflect on the effectiveness of your unconventional approach. Did it lead to a better outcome or reveal new insights? Consider how embracing incongruence can help you adapt to changing conditions and achieve success in various contexts.

Motivation

"The most difficult and rewarding victories are those from which we learn the most."

CHAPTER 12

***

Chapter Summary

The Balance Of Specialization And Interdisciplinary Thinking In Scientific Discovery

OLIVER SMITHIES, A molecular biochemist, revolutionized biology and chemistry with his invention of gel electrophoresis. His enthusiasm for experimentation extended beyond the lab, as he encouraged students to explore laterally and diversify their experiences.

Tu Youyou, the first Chinese Nobel Laureate in Physiology or Medicine, made a groundbreaking discovery by experimenting with artemisinin, leading to one of the most significant drug discoveries in history. Her outsider perspective allowed her to explore unconventional avenues.

Scientists like Andre Geim, Konstantin Novoselov, and Arturo Casadevall advocate for a balance between specialization and interdisciplinary thinking in scientific inquiry. They believe that the future of discovery depends on this balance.

Challenges To Interdisciplinary Research

Despite the recognized importance of interdisciplinary research, several challenges hinder its progress:

- Lack of Funding:

Research that combines different fields often struggles to secure funding due to its perceived lack of focus.

- Publication Bias:

Interdisciplinary research may face bias in publication, as traditional journals often favor specialized studies.

- Institutional Barriers:

The current academic structure promotes specialization and compartmentalization, making it difficult for researchers from different fields to collaborate effectively.

The Importance Of Diversity And Inefficiency

Laszlo Casadevall emphasizes the need to maintain diversity and inefficiency in the innovation ecosystem. He believes that truly groundbreaking discoveries often arise from unexpected connections between seemingly unrelated fields.

Conclusion

The balance between specialization and interdisciplinary thinking is crucial for scientific progress. Encouraging diverse perspectives, promoting collaboration across disciplines, and valuing inefficiency in the pursuit of knowledge are essential to fostering a vibrant and innovative scientific landscape.

Key Takeaways And Learning

1. Oliver Smithies discovered gel electrophoresis by replacing paper with moist starch grains, transforming biology and chemistry.

2. Smithies encouraged pupils to explore laterally, diversify their experience, and establish their own path in the pursuit of match quality.

3. Tu Youyou, the first Chinese native to receive the Nobel Prize in Physiology or Medicine, discovered artemisinin, a significant drug discovery.

4. Tu had an outsider advantage, allowing her to explore areas others would not.

5. Andre Geim Novoselov and Arturo Casadevall advocate for balancing the cult of the head start with mental meandering, broad conceptual talents, and interdisciplinary cross-fertilization.

6. Casadevall warns that scientific research is in danger, with progress decreasing and retractions increasing.

7. Casadevall and Gundula Bosch are de-specializing student training with multidisciplinary courses.

8. Doctors and scientists often lack basic reasoning abilities, leading to a system of parallel trenches across various fields.

9. The modern structure of specialization and intellectual archipelagos impedes a comprehensive understanding of complex systems.

10. Networks that encourage the establishment of successful teams have permeable boundaries, while unsuccessful teams are divided into small, isolated clusters.

11. Human creativity is an "import/export business of ideas," and effective teams often include more diverse individuals.

12. Scientists who have worked overseas are more likely to make significant scientific contributions.

13. Studies show that work connecting different pieces of information is less likely to be funded, published in prestigious journals, and neglected after publication.

14. Laszlo Casadevall believes the innovation ecosystem should purposely maintain diversity and inefficiency.

15. Hyperspecialization is limited to carefully defined, kind learning contexts, and much of pushing boundaries is inefficient.

16. Casadevall argues that communication occurs during carpooling.

Questions To Think About

1. How can you encourage yourself to explore laterally, diversify your experience, and establish your own path in the pursuit of match quality?

_____

_____

_____

_____

_____

_____

_____

2. What are the advantages of being an outsider in a field of study?

_____

_____

_____

_____

_____

_____

_____

3. How can you balance the cult of the head start in scientific inquiry with mental meandering, extensive experience, broad conceptual talents, and interdisciplinary cross-fertilization?

_____

_____

_____

_____

_____

_____

_____

4. What are some of the challenges facing scientific research today?

_____

_____

_____

_____

_____

_____

_____

5. How can we create a more diverse and inclusive scientific community?

_____

_____

_____

_____

_____

_____

_____

6. How can we encourage scientists to think more creatively and take more risks?

_____

_____

_____

_____

_____

_____

7. What is the role of inefficiency in the innovation ecosystem?

_____

_____

_____

_____

_____

_____

8. How can we create an innovation ecosystem that is both diverse and efficient?

_____

_____

_____

_____

_____

_____

_____

9. What are some of the challenges facing the innovation ecosystem today?

_____

_____

_____

_____

_____

_____

_____

10. How can we overcome these challenges and create a more innovative future?

_____

_____

_____

_____

_____

_____

_____

Personal Growth Activities

1. Diversify Your Experience:

• *Action:*

Seek out opportunities to work in different fields, industries, or disciplines, even if it's just for a short time.

• *Exercise:*

Take a class in a subject you know nothing about, or volunteer in a field unrelated to your current work.

• *Analysis:*

Reflect on how these new experiences have expanded your perspective and understanding of the world.

2. Embrace Lateral Thinking:

• *Action:*

Challenge yourself to think creatively and come up with unconventional solutions to problems.

• *Exercise:*

Try brainstorming sessions where you encourage wild ideas and off-the-wall thinking.

• *Analysis:*

Evaluate the ideas generated and see if any have potential for innovation or improvement.

3. Foster Interdisciplinary Collaboration:

• *Action:*

Seek out opportunities to collaborate with people from different backgrounds and disciplines.

• *Exercise:*

Join interdisciplinary research teams or projects, or attend conferences and workshops that bring together experts from diverse fields.

• *Analysis:*

Reflect on how interdisciplinary collaboration has enriched your understanding of a problem and led to new insights or solutions.

Motivation

"The future of discovery is dependent on a balance between mental meandering, extensive experience, broad conceptual talents, and interdisciplinary cross-fertilization."

CONCLUSION

***

Chapter Summary

Navigating The Paradox Of Breadth And Specialization: A Path To Success

IN THE PURSUIT of success, conventional wisdom often dictates a narrow focus, minimizing distractions and pursuing specialized expertise. However, the author challenges this "Tiger path," arguing that it oversimplifies the reality of breakthrough invention.

Breakthroughs are highly unpredictable and require more than just a tolerance for failure. History is replete with examples of notable inventors, from Thomas Edison to Shakespeare and Rachel Whiteread, who achieved greatness through experimentation and diverse experiences.

The author emphasizes that breakthrough invention is a difficult and inconsistent process, lacking a clear method or precise feedback system. Accepting this inherent diversity and embracing specialization is crucial for success.

In systems that demand hyperspecialization, the author advocates for embracing breadth, diversified experience, and interdisciplinary exploration. They cite examples of athletes and musicians who often have broad early experience and delayed specialization, challenging the notion that early hyperspecialization is necessary for skill development.

The author encourages individuals not to feel behind and to approach their personal journeys and objectives with a willingness to learn and adapt. They emphasize that specialization is not inherently bad and that mental wandering and personal exploration can be sources of power.

In essence, the author presents a more comprehensive and realistic perspective on the path to success, recognizing the value of both breadth and specialization in a world that is constantly evolving and demanding diverse skill sets.

Key Takeaways And Learning

1. The "Tiger path" to success, which emphasizes narrow focus and minimization of distractions, is not always the best approach.

2. Breakthroughs are highly variable and require more than just a tolerance for failure.

3. Notable inventors and artists, such as Thomas Edison, Shakespeare, and Rachel Whiteread, achieved success through experimentation and exploration of diverse fields.

4. Breakthrough invention is difficult and inconsistent, with no clear method or precise feedback system.

5. Accepting diversity and specialization is critical for success in many fields.

6. Embracing breadth, diversified experience, and interdisciplinary exploration is valuable in systems that require hyperspecialization.

7. Many athletes and musicians have broad early experience and delayed specialization, suggesting that early hyperspecialization is not necessary for skill development.

8. It's important to not feel behind and to approach personal journeys and objectives with a willingness to learn and adapt.

9. Specialization is not necessarily bad, and mental wandering and personal exploration can be sources of power.

Questions To Think About

1. Reflect on your own career or educational journey. Have you pursued a Tiger path or a more diverse and exploratory path?

_____

_____

_____

_____

_____

_____

_____

What have been the benefits and challenges of your approach?

_____

_____

_____

_____

_____

_____

_____

2. Consider the examples of Thomas Edison, Shakespeare, and Rachel Whiteread. How did their breadth of experience and experimentation contribute to their success?

_____

_____

_____

_____

_____

_____

_____

3. What are some examples of systems that require hyperspecialization?

_____

_____

_____

_____

_____

_____

_____

How can diversity and specialization be balanced in these systems?

_____

_____

_____

_____

_____

_____

_____

4. Think about athletes and musicians who have achieved success. What role did broad early experience and delayed specialization play in their development?

_____

_____

_____

_____

_____

_____

5. How can you approach your personal journey and objectives with a willingness to learn and adapt?

_____

_____

_____

_____

_____

_____

_____

What are some strategies for embracing change and exploration?

_____

_____

_____

_____

_____

_____

_____

6. Reflect on the idea that specialization is not necessarily bad. How can you leverage your specialized knowledge and skills while also maintaining a sense of curiosity and openness to new experiences?

_____

_____

_____

_____

_____

_____

_____

7. Consider the concept of mental wandering and personal exploration as sources of power. How can you create space in your life for these activities?

_____

_____

_____

_____

_____

_____

_____

What are some ways to harness their potential for creativity and innovation?

_____

_____

_____

_____

_____

_____

_____

Personal Growth Activities

1. Embrace Diverse Experiences:

• *Action:*

Make a list of your interests, skills, and experiences, both inside and outside your current field of expertise. Consider activities you enjoyed in the past, hobbies you've put on hold, or new areas you're curious about.

• *Exercise:*

Set aside time each week to explore these diverse interests. Take classes, attend workshops, join clubs, or simply read books and articles on topics that intrigue you.

• *Analysis:*

Reflect on how these experiences broaden your perspective and contribute to your overall development. Consider how they might connect with your current pursuits or inspire new ideas.

2. Experiment And Tinker:

• *Action:*

Dedicate a specific time each week to experimentation and creative play. This could involve working on personal projects, exploring new techniques or approaches in your field, or simply setting aside time to brainstorm and generate ideas.

• *Exercise:*

Choose a topic or problem that interests you and spend some time experimenting with different solutions. Don't be afraid to fail or make mistakes; view them as learning opportunities.

• *Analysis:*

Reflect on what you learned from the experimentation process. Did you gain new insights? Discover new possibilities? Challenge your assumptions?

3. Seek Interdisciplinary Connections:

• *Action:*

Make an effort to connect with people from different fields and backgrounds. Attend conferences, workshops, or events where you can interact with individuals from diverse disciplines.

• *Exercise:*

Initiate conversations with people whose work or interests differ from your own. Ask questions, listen to their perspectives, and explore potential collaborations.

• *Analysis:*

Reflect on how these interdisciplinary interactions expand your thinking and open up new possibilities for innovation and problem-solving. Consider how you might incorporate insights from other fields into your own work.

Motivation

"Embrace breadth and diversity in your pursuits; specialization can come later."

WE LOVE FEEDBACK

✳✳✳

Dear Book Spark Readers,

Thank you so much for choosing our workbook! We're happy you decided to invest in your learning and growth, and we hope that you've found our workbook helpful and informative.

We know you have many choices regarding workbooks, and we appreciate you trusting us to help you on your journey. We put a lot of thought and effort into creating our workbooks, and we're always looking for ways to improve.

Thats why we're asking for your honest feedback. Please take a few minutes to leave a review of your experience with our workbook on Amazon. Your feedback is invaluable to us, and it helps us to create better workbooks for other readers in the future.

In addition, we encourage you to follow our author profile on Amazon. This way, you'll be notified whenever we release a new workbook. We're also happy to take requests for workbooks on specific books. So, if you have a book in mind that you'd like to see a workbook for, please let us know in your review.

Again, thank you for choosing Book Spark! We're grateful for your support.

Sincerely,

The Book Spark Team

P.S. Remember to leave a review! Every review helps us to create better workbooks for readers.

Made in the USA
Las Vegas, NV
03 May 2024

89490469R00089